Welcome!

This Biblical Meditation Series is designed to help you meditate through the entire Bible in about three years. The series will help you read through each chapter of the Bible at a pace that allows you to meditate, apply, pray, and enjoy your time in the Word. At the end of the series, you will have created your own personal commentary of your time spent in the Bible.

The series continues with Volume Three. In this volume we will read through the books of Numbers, John, and Deuteronomy as we work through the Bible alternating Old and New Testament books. Each volume will take you through approximately a quarter of a year but can be started at any time.

Each day you work in this book, you will read the chapter (or short chapters) written at the top of the page, then you'll fill in each of the boxes on the two-page spread for that day. There are six days of regular work, then on every seventh day there are two pages for reflection on the previous week's work.

In each box, you'll see questions going down the left side of the boxes and different ones on the right. Choose which side of questions you'll work through depending on the chapter. If there is a verse that really stands out in the chapter, then use the questions on the left. If the chapter is more narrative in structure (tells a story) then use the questions on the right. If neither of these apply, use the bookmark on the next page.

My hope and prayer is that as you work through these pages you'll have time to slow down and think deeply about the truth in the Bible and how it teaches us about God and His redemptive plan and how it applies to your life and your growth as His child.

Find out more at: www.stonesoupforfive.com or join a group of people working through this together on Facebook at:
www.facebook.com/groups/journalanddoodle/
or
follow my Facebook page at:
www.facebook.com/StoneSoupForFive/

Cut out and use this
bookmark for the hard,
descriptive chapters.

You'll still be able to think
through the chapter in a
different way!

If you'd like a printable copy
(to print on cardstock) you
can find the file at my
website
www.stonesoupforfive.com
Be sure to subscribe for
access to all the bonuses!

Bible Reading and Meditation Journal

the hard chapters

Summarize
(keep this box the same)

I notice...
(replaces: Verses that stood out, box two)
Write out anything you notice
in the chapter. Anything at all.

I wonder...
(replaces: Why did I pick this verse, box three)
Is there anything you are curious about?
Anything you don't understand?
Anything you wonder about in the chapter?

I'm reminded of...
(replaces: Definitions of words, box four)
Were you reminded of anything when
you read through the chapter?
A story (real life or in the Bible)?
A verse?

Continue with the rest
of the boxes as written
(using the questions
on the right of box five).

www.stonesoupforfive.com

the book of Numbers preview

Before you start diving into the book of Numbers, take sometime to learn about it, where it fits into the overall narrative of the Bible, and key themes to look for.

At the beginning of each new book of the Bible, I've included two preview pages for you to use to journal and take notes.

Read the introduction to the book of Numbers in your Bible and jot down any notes.

There are some EXCELLENT videos on TheBibleProject.com or on their YouTube channel. On their website you can even print out a copy of their drawing (I shrink it down and print it out and tape it into my guide on the preview page). View the videos on the Bible project and also read the introduction at the beginning of the book in your Bible. They also have lots of other great resources, including podcasts talking about books of the Bible, so spend some time browsing around their site.

If you want to go even further, there are great free commentaries online to look up too. Here are some I love:

From Grace to You:
https://www.gty.org/library/bible-introductions

From Precept Austin:
http://www.preceptaustin.org/bybook

and Blue Letter Bible:
https://www.blueletterbible.org/resources/intros.cfm

Numbers preview notes

Map courtesy of Blue Letter Bible. Used with permission.

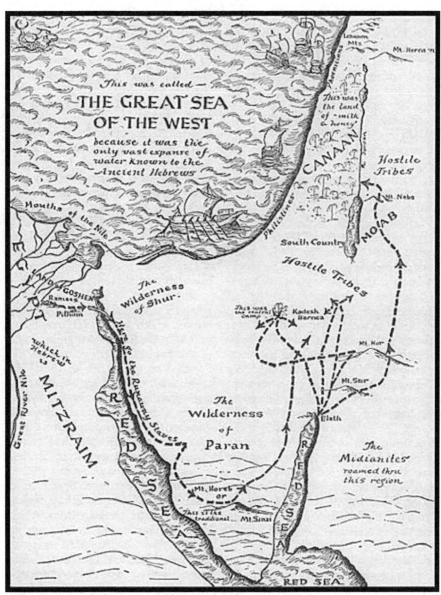

Map courtesy of Blue Letter Bible. Used with permission.

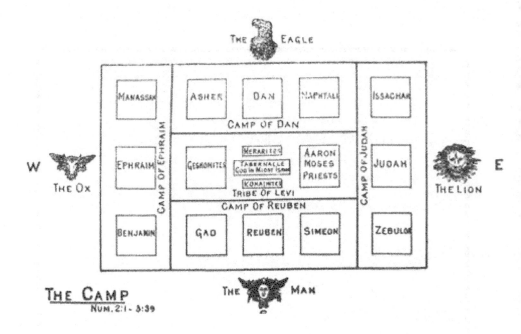

THE EAGLE

W — THE OX

E — THE LION

THE MAN

THE CAMP
Num. 2:1 - 3:39

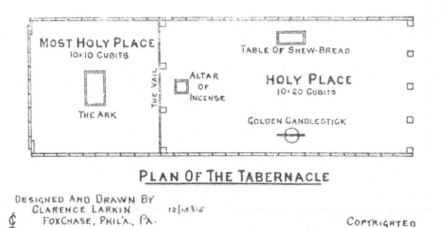

PLAN OF THE TABERNACLE

DESIGNED AND DRAWN BY CLARENCE LARKIN
FOXCHASE, PHIL'A, PA.
12|15|16
COPYRIGHTED

Images courtesy of Blue Letter Bible and Clarence Larkin. Used with permission.

Image courtesy of Blue Letter Bible and Clarence Larkin. Used with permission.

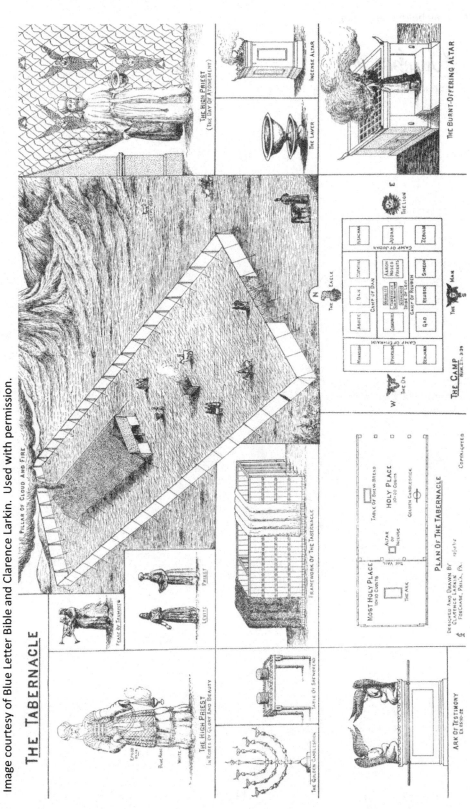

Numbers 1

Date:

Summarize the main idea(s) in this chapter:

Verse(s) that stood out   or   Who is in this chapter?
What do they say? What do they do?

Why did I pick this verse?   or   What is going on?
Is there anything going wrong?

Definitions of words and/or   or   When and where
cross references from my verse   did this happen?

Rewrite the verse in your own words   or   Why is this chapter in the Bible?
or personalize it.   Why did these events happen?
                                                                               Why did the people act this way?

Does this verse reveal anything about God/Jesus/Holy Spirit?
Are there examples to follow or avoid? What does this chapter have to teach me?

How can I apply insights from this verse today? This week?

Notes, quotes, doodles, checklists, prayers, etc.

#Iwillmeditate

Numbers 2

Date:

Summarize the main idea(s) in this chapter:

Verse(s) that stood out   or   Who is in this chapter?
What do they say? What do they do?

Why did I pick this verse?   or   What is going on?
Is there anything going wrong?

Definitions of words and/or   or   When and where
cross references from my verse   did this happen?

Rewrite the verse in your own words or personalize it.   or   Why is this chapter in the Bible?
Why did these events happen?
Why did the people act this way?

Does this verse reveal anything about God/Jesus/Holy Spirit?
Are there examples to follow or avoid? What does this chapter have to teach me?

How can I apply insights from this verse today? This week?

Notes, quotes, doodles, checklists, prayers, etc.

#Iwillmeditate

Numbers 3

Date:

Summarize the main idea(s) in this chapter:

Verse(s) that stood out   or   Who is in this chapter?
What do they say? What do they do?

Why did I pick this verse?   or   What is going on?
Is there anything going wrong?

Definitions of words and/or   or   When and where
cross references from my verse   did this happen?

Rewrite the verse in your own words   or   Why is this chapter in the Bible?
or personalize it.   Why did these events happen?
                                                                            Why did the people act this way?

Does this verse reveal anything about God/Jesus/Holy Spirit?
Are there examples to follow or avoid? What does this chapter have to teach me?

How can I apply insights from this verse today? This week?

Notes, quotes, doodles, checklists, prayers, etc.

#Iwillmeditate

Numbers 4

Date:

Summarize the main idea(s) in this chapter:

Verse(s) that stood out   or   Who is in this chapter?
What do they say? What do they do?

Why did I pick this verse?   or   What is going on?
Is there anything going wrong?

Definitions of words and/or   or   When and where
cross references from my verse   did this happen?

Rewrite the verse in your own words or personalize it.

or

Why is this chapter in the Bible?
Why did these events happen?
Why did the people act this way?

Does this verse reveal anything about God/Jesus/Holy Spirit?
Are there examples to follow or avoid? What does this chapter have to teach me?

How can I apply insights from this verse today? This week?

Notes, quotes, doodles, checklists, prayers, etc.

#Iwillmeditate

Numbers 5

Date:

Summarize the main idea(s) in this chapter:

Verse(s) that stood out   or   Who is in this chapter?
What do they say? What do they do?

Why did I pick this verse?   or   What is going on?
Is there anything going wrong?

Definitions of words and/or   or   When and where
cross references from my verse   did this happen?

Rewrite the verse in your own words   or   Why is this chapter in the Bible?
or personalize it.   Why did these events happen?
                                                                        Why did the people act this way?

Does this verse reveal anything about God/Jesus/Holy Spirit?
Are there examples to follow or avoid? What does this chapter have to teach me?

How can I apply insights from this verse today? This week?

Notes, quotes, doodles, checklists, prayers, etc.

#Iwillmeditate

Numbers 6

Date:

Summarize the main idea(s) in this chapter:

Verse(s) that stood out   or   Who is in this chapter?
What do they say? What do they do?

Why did I pick this verse?   or   What is going on?
Is there anything going wrong?

Definitions of words and/or   or   When and where
cross references from my verse   did this happen?

Rewrite the verse in your own words   or   Why is this chapter in the Bible?
or personalize it.   Why did these events happen?
                                                            Why did the people act this way?

Does this verse reveal anything about God/Jesus/Holy Spirit?
Are there examples to follow or avoid? What does this chapter have to teach me?

How can I apply insights from this verse today? This week?

Notes, quotes, doodles, checklists, prayers, etc.

Review and reflect #29

Date:

Review each of the last six days work. Write or list the main takeaway you got from each chapter. (Look closely at the sections "What does this reveal about God?" and "How can I apply this?")

Are there any themes showing up in this week's work?

Are there any areas God is wanting to grow my faith or trust?
Are there any insights from this week's work on how to do this?

Are there any sins God is spotlighting in my life?
Are there any insights from this week's work on how to kill these sins?

Re-read one or two of the most impactful verses from this week and turn them into a prayer. (There is room on the next pages to write it down if you want.)

How can I thank or praise God as a result of what I've learned this week?

How can I apply what I've learned this week to my life today and next week?

Where do I need His strength for today? Tomorrow? Next week?

Is there a verse from this week that I should commit to memory? Write it on the next page or on a 3x5 card to take with you to memorize.

Are there any sins I need to confess to God in prayer?

Is there anyone I need to forgive? Is there anyone I need to ask forgiveness of?

Are there any seeds of bitterness starting to take root in my heart?

Are there any fears or worries I need to lay at His feet?

notes, verses to memorize

prayers, doodles, etc

Numbers 7

Date:

Summarize the main idea(s) in this chapter:

Verse(s) that stood out   or   Who is in this chapter?
What do they say? What do they do?

Why did I pick this verse?   or   What is going on?
Is there anything going wrong?

Definitions of words and/or   or   When and where
cross references from my verse   did this happen?

Rewrite the verse in your own words   or   Why is this chapter in the Bible?
or personalize it.   Why did these events happen?
                                              Why did the people act this way?

Does this verse reveal anything about God/Jesus/Holy Spirit?
Are there examples to follow or avoid? What does this chapter have to teach me?

How can I apply insights from this verse today? This week?

Notes, quotes, doodles, checklists, prayers, etc.

Numbers 8

Date:

Summarize the main idea(s) in this chapter:

Verse(s) that stood out   or   Who is in this chapter?
What do they say? What do they do?

Why did I pick this verse?   or   What is going on?
Is there anything going wrong?

Definitions of words and/or   or   When and where
cross references from my verse   did this happen?

Rewrite the verse in your own words   or   Why is this chapter in the Bible?
or personalize it.   Why did these events happen?
                                                                        Why did the people act this way?

Does this verse reveal anything about God/Jesus/Holy Spirit?
Are there examples to follow or avoid? What does this chapter have to teach me?

How can I apply insights from this verse today? This week?

Notes, quotes, doodles, checklists, prayers, etc.

#Iwillmeditate

Numbers 9

Date:

Summarize the main idea(s) in this chapter:

Verse(s) that stood out   or   Who is in this chapter?
What do they say? What do they do?

Why did I pick this verse?   or   What is going on?
Is there anything going wrong?

Definitions of words and/or   or   When and where
cross references from my verse   did this happen?

Rewrite the verse in your own words   or   Why is this chapter in the Bible?
or personalize it.   Why did these events happen?
                                                                   Why did the people act this way?

Does this verse reveal anything about God/Jesus/Holy Spirit?
Are there examples to follow or avoid? What does this chapter have to teach me?

How can I apply insights from this verse today? This week?

Notes, quotes, doodles, checklists, prayers, etc.

#Iwillmeditate

Numbers 10

Date:

Summarize the main idea(s) in this chapter:

Verse(s) that stood out   or   Who is in this chapter?
What do they say? What do they do?

Why did I pick this verse?   or   What is going on?
Is there anything going wrong?

Definitions of words and/or   or   When and where
cross references from my verse   did this happen?

Rewrite the verse in your own words   or   Why is this chapter in the Bible?
or personalize it.   Why did these events happen?
                                                                            Why did the people act this way?

Does this verse reveal anything about God/Jesus/Holy Spirit?
Are there examples to follow or avoid? What does this chapter have to teach me?

How can I apply insights from this verse today? This week?

Notes, quotes, doodles, checklists, prayers, etc.

#Iwillmeditate

Numbers 11

Date:

Summarize the main idea(s) in this chapter:

Verse(s) that stood out   or   Who is in this chapter?
What do they say? What do they do?

Why did I pick this verse?   or   What is going on?
Is there anything going wrong?

Definitions of words and/or   or   When and where
cross references from my verse   did this happen?

Rewrite the verse in your own words   or   Why is this chapter in the Bible?
or personalize it.   Why did these events happen?
                                                           Why did the people act this way?

Does this verse reveal anything about God/Jesus/Holy Spirit?
Are there examples to follow or avoid? What does this chapter have to teach me?

How can I apply insights from this verse today? This week?

Notes, quotes, doodles, checklists, prayers, etc.

Numbers 12

Date:

Summarize the main idea(s) in this chapter:

Verse(s) that stood out   or   Who is in this chapter?
What do they say? What do they do?

Why did I pick this verse?   or   What is going on?
Is there anything going wrong?

Definitions of words and/or   or   When and where
cross references from my verse   did this happen?

Rewrite the verse in your own words or personalize it.

or

Why is this chapter in the Bible?
Why did these events happen?
Why did the people act this way?

Does this verse reveal anything about God/Jesus/Holy Spirit?
Are there examples to follow or avoid? What does this chapter have to teach me?

How can I apply insights from this verse today? This week?

Notes, quotes, doodles, checklists, prayers, etc.

#Iwillmeditate

Review and reflect #30

Date:

Review each of the last six days work. Write or list the main takeaway you got from each chapter. (Look closely at the sections "What does this reveal about God?" and "How can I apply this?")

Are there any themes showing up in this week's work?

Are there any areas God is wanting to grow my faith or trust?
Are there any insights from this week's work on how to do this?

Are there any sins God is spotlighting in my life?
Are there any insights from this week's work on how to kill these sins?

Re-read one or two of the most impactful verses from this week and turn them into a prayer. (There is room on the next pages to write it down if you want.)

How can I thank or praise God as a result of what I've learned this week?

How can I apply what I've learned this week to my life today and next week?

Where do I need His strength for today? Tomorrow? Next week?

Is there a verse from this week that I should commit to memory? Write it on the next page or on a 3x5 card to take with you to memorize.

Are there any sins I need to confess to God in prayer?

Is there anyone I need to forgive? Is there anyone I need to ask forgiveness of?

Are there any seeds of bitterness starting to take root in my heart?

Are there any fears or worries I need to lay at His feet?

#Iwillmeditate

notes, verses to memorize

prayers, doodles, etc

Numbers 13

Date:

Summarize the main idea(s) in this chapter:

Verse(s) that stood out   or   Who is in this chapter?
What do they say? What do they do?

Why did I pick this verse?   or   What is going on?
Is there anything going wrong?

Definitions of words and/or   or   When and where
cross references from my verse   did this happen?

Rewrite the verse in your own words or personalize it.

or

Why is this chapter in the Bible?
Why did these events happen?
Why did the people act this way?

Does this verse reveal anything about God/Jesus/Holy Spirit?
Are there examples to follow or avoid? What does this chapter have to teach me?

How can I apply insights from this verse today? This week?

Notes, quotes, doodles, checklists, prayers, etc.

Numbers 14

Date:

Summarize the main idea(s) in this chapter:

Verse(s) that stood out   or   Who is in this chapter?
What do they say? What do they do?

Why did I pick this verse?   or   What is going on?
Is there anything going wrong?

Definitions of words and/or   or   When and where
cross references from my verse   did this happen?

Rewrite the verse in your own words   or   Why is this chapter in the Bible?
or personalize it.   Why did these events happen?
                                                                                  Why did the people act this way?

Does this verse reveal anything about God/Jesus/Holy Spirit?
Are there examples to follow or avoid? What does this chapter have to teach me?

How can I apply insights from this verse today? This week?

Notes, quotes, doodles, checklists, prayers, etc.

#Iwillmeditate

Numbers 15

Date:

Summarize the main idea(s) in this chapter:

Verse(s) that stood out   or   Who is in this chapter?
What do they say? What do they do?

Why did I pick this verse?   or   What is going on?
Is there anything going wrong?

Definitions of words and/or   or   When and where
cross references from my verse   did this happen?

Rewrite the verse in your own words or personalize it.   or   Why is this chapter in the Bible? Why did these events happen? Why did the people act this way?

Does this verse reveal anything about God/Jesus/Holy Spirit? Are there examples to follow or avoid? What does this chapter have to teach me?

How can I apply insights from this verse today? This week?

Notes, quotes, doodles, checklists, prayers, etc.

Numbers 16

Date:

Summarize the main idea(s) in this chapter:

Verse(s) that stood out   or   Who is in this chapter?
What do they say? What do they do?

Why did I pick this verse?   or   What is going on?
Is there anything going wrong?

Definitions of words and/or   or   When and where
cross references from my verse   did this happen?

Rewrite the verse in your own words   or   Why is this chapter in the Bible?
or personalize it.   Why did these events happen?
                                                                    Why did the people act this way?

Does this verse reveal anything about God/Jesus/Holy Spirit?
Are there examples to follow or avoid? What does this chapter have to teach me?

How can I apply insights from this verse today? This week?

Notes, quotes, doodles, checklists, prayers, etc.

Numbers 17-18

Date:

Summarize the main idea(s) in this chapter:

Verse(s) that stood out   or   Who is in this chapter?
What do they say? What do they do?

Why did I pick this verse?   or   What is going on?
Is there anything going wrong?

Definitions of words and/or   or   When and where
cross references from my verse   did this happen?

Rewrite the verse in your own words or personalize it.

or

Why is this chapter in the Bible?
Why did these events happen?
Why did the people act this way?

Does this verse reveal anything about God/Jesus/Holy Spirit?
Are there examples to follow or avoid? What does this chapter have to teach me?

How can I apply insights from this verse today? This week?

Notes, quotes, doodles, checklists, prayers, etc.

#Iwillmeditate

Numbers 19-20

Date:

Summarize the main idea(s) in this chapter:

Verse(s) that stood out   or   Who is in this chapter?
What do they say? What do they do?

Why did I pick this verse?   or   What is going on?
Is there anything going wrong?

Definitions of words and/or   or   When and where
cross references from my verse   did this happen?

Rewrite the verse in your own words or personalize it.   or   Why is this chapter in the Bible?
Why did these events happen?
Why did the people act this way?

Does this verse reveal anything about God/Jesus/Holy Spirit?
Are there examples to follow or avoid? What does this chapter have to teach me?

How can I apply insights from this verse today? This week?

Notes, quotes, doodles, checklists, prayers, etc.

#Iwillmeditate

Review and reflect #31

Date:

Review each of the last six days work. Write or list the main takeaway you got from each chapter. (Look closely at the sections "What does this reveal about God?" and "How can I apply this?")

Are there any themes showing up in this week's work?

Are there any areas God is wanting to grow my faith or trust?
Are there any insights from this week's work on how to do this?

Are there any sins God is spotlighting in my life?
Are there any insights from this week's work on how to kill these sins?

Re-read one or two of the most impactful verses from this week and turn them into a prayer. (There is room on the next pages to write it down if you want.)

How can I thank or praise God as a result of what I've learned this week?

How can I apply what I've learned this week to my life today and next week?

Where do I need His strength for today? Tomorrow? Next week?

Is there a verse from this week that I should commit to memory? Write it on the next page or on a 3x5 card to take with you to memorize.

Are there any sins I need to confess to God in prayer?

Is there anyone I need to forgive? Is there anyone I need to ask forgiveness of?

Are there any seeds of bitterness starting to take root in my heart?

Are there any fears or worries I need to lay at His feet?

#Iwillmeditate

notes, verses to memorize

prayers, doodles, etc

Numbers 21

Date:

Summarize the main idea(s) in this chapter:

Verse(s) that stood out　　　　　or　　　　　Who is in this chapter?
What do they say? What do they do?

Why did I pick this verse?　　　　or　　　　　What is going on?
Is there anything going wrong?

Definitions of words and/or　　　　or　　　　When and where
cross references from my verse　　　　　　　did this happen?

Rewrite the verse in your own words
or personalize it.

or

Why is this chapter in the Bible?
Why did these events happen?
Why did the people act this way?

Does this verse reveal anything about God/Jesus/Holy Spirit?
Are there examples to follow or avoid? What does this chapter have to teach me?

How can I apply insights from this verse today? This week?

Notes, quotes, doodles, checklists, prayers, etc.

#Iwillmeditate

Numbers 22

Date:

Summarize the main idea(s) in this chapter:

Verse(s) that stood out   or   Who is in this chapter?
What do they say? What do they do?

Why did I pick this verse?   or   What is going on?
Is there anything going wrong?

Definitions of words and/or   or   When and where
cross references from my verse   did this happen?

Rewrite the verse in your own words or personalize it.

or

Why is this chapter in the Bible?
Why did these events happen?
Why did the people act this way?

Does this verse reveal anything about God/Jesus/Holy Spirit?
Are there examples to follow or avoid? What does this chapter have to teach me?

How can I apply insights from this verse today? This week?

Notes, quotes, doodles, checklists, prayers, etc.

#Iwillmeditate

Numbers 23

Date:

Summarize the main idea(s) in this chapter:

Verse(s) that stood out   or   Who is in this chapter?
What do they say? What do they do?

Why did I pick this verse?   or   What is going on?
Is there anything going wrong?

Definitions of words and/or   or   When and where
cross references from my verse   did this happen?

Rewrite the verse in your own words   or   Why is this chapter in the Bible?
or personalize it.   Why did these events happen?
                                                 Why did the people act this way?

Does this verse reveal anything about God/Jesus/Holy Spirit?
Are there examples to follow or avoid? What does this chapter have to teach me?

How can I apply insights from this verse today? This week?

Notes, quotes, doodles, checklists, prayers, etc.

#Iwillmeditate

Numbers 24-25

Date:

Summarize the main idea(s) in this chapter:

Verse(s) that stood out   or   Who is in this chapter?
                                             What do they say? What do they do?

Why did I pick this verse?   or   What is going on?
                                                Is there anything going wrong?

Definitions of words and/or   or   When and where
cross references from my verse   did this happen?

Rewrite the verse in your own words   or   Why is this chapter in the Bible?
or personalize it.   Why did these events happen?
                                                                  Why did the people act this way?

Does this verse reveal anything about God/Jesus/Holy Spirit?
Are there examples to follow or avoid? What does this chapter have to teach me?

How can I apply insights from this verse today? This week?

Notes, quotes, doodles, checklists, prayers, etc.

#Iwillmeditate

Numbers 26

Date:

Summarize the main idea(s) in this chapter:

Verse(s) that stood out   or   Who is in this chapter?
What do they say? What do they do?

Why did I pick this verse?   or   What is going on?
Is there anything going wrong?

Definitions of words and/or   or   When and where
cross references from my verse   did this happen?

Rewrite the verse in your own words   or   Why is this chapter in the Bible?
or personalize it.   Why did these events happen?
                                                                       Why did the people act this way?

Does this verse reveal anything about God/Jesus/Holy Spirit?
Are there examples to follow or avoid? What does this chapter have to teach me?

How can I apply insights from this verse today? This week?

Notes, quotes, doodles, checklists, prayers, etc.

71

Numbers 27

Date:

Summarize the main idea(s) in this chapter:

Verse(s) that stood out   or   Who is in this chapter?
What do they say? What do they do?

Why did I pick this verse?   or   What is going on?
Is there anything going wrong?

Definitions of words and/or   or   When and where
cross references from my verse   did this happen?

Rewrite the verse in your own words
or personalize it.

or

Why is this chapter in the Bible?
Why did these events happen?
Why did the people act this way?

Does this verse reveal anything about God/Jesus/Holy Spirit?
Are there examples to follow or avoid? What does this chapter have to teach me?

How can I apply insights from this verse today? This week?

Notes, quotes, doodles, checklists, prayers, etc.

#Iwillmeditate

Review and reflect #32

Date:

Review each of the last six days work. Write or list the main takeaway you got from each chapter. (Look closely at the sections "What does this reveal about God?" and "How can I apply this?")

Are there any themes showing up in this week's work?

Are there any areas God is wanting to grow my faith or trust?
Are there any insights from this week's work on how to do this?

Are there any sins God is spotlighting in my life?
Are there any insights from this week's work on how to kill these sins?

Re-read one or two of the most impactful verses from this week and turn them into a prayer. (There is room on the next pages to write it down if you want.)

How can I thank or praise God as a result of what I've learned this week?

How can I apply what I've learned this week to my life today and next week?

Where do I need His strength for today? Tomorrow? Next week?

Is there a verse from this week that I should commit to memory? Write it on the next page or on a 3x5 card to take with you to memorize.

Are there any sins I need to confess to God in prayer?

Is there anyone I need to forgive? Is there anyone I need to ask forgiveness of?

Are there any seeds of bitterness starting to take root in my heart?

Are there any fears or worries I need to lay at His feet?

#Iwillmeditate

notes, verses to memorize

prayers, doodles, etc

Numbers 28

Date:

Summarize the main idea(s) in this chapter:

Verse(s) that stood out   or   Who is in this chapter?
What do they say? What do they do?

Why did I pick this verse?   or   What is going on?
Is there anything going wrong?

Definitions of words and/or   or   When and where
cross references from my verse   did this happen?

Rewrite the verse in your own words or personalize it.

or

Why is this chapter in the Bible? Why did these events happen? Why did the people act this way?

Does this verse reveal anything about God/Jesus/Holy Spirit?
Are there examples to follow or avoid? What does this chapter have to teach me?

How can I apply insights from this verse today? This week?

Notes, quotes, doodles, checklists, prayers, etc.

Numbers 29

Date:

Summarize the main idea(s) in this chapter:

Verse(s) that stood out   or   Who is in this chapter?
                                              What do they say? What do they do?

Why did I pick this verse?   or   What is going on?
                                                Is there anything going wrong?

Definitions of words and/or   or   When and where
cross references from my verse   did this happen?

Rewrite the verse in your own words or personalize it.

or

Why is this chapter in the Bible?
Why did these events happen?
Why did the people act this way?

Does this verse reveal anything about God/Jesus/Holy Spirit?
Are there examples to follow or avoid? What does this chapter have to teach me?

How can I apply insights from this verse today? This week?

Notes, quotes, doodles, checklists, prayers, etc.

#Iwillmeditate

Numbers 30

Date:

Summarize the main idea(s) in this chapter:

Verse(s) that stood out   or   Who is in this chapter?
What do they say? What do they do?

Why did I pick this verse?   or   What is going on?
Is there anything going wrong?

Definitions of words and/or   or   When and where
cross references from my verse   did this happen?

Rewrite the verse in your own words   or   Why is this chapter in the Bible?
or personalize it.   Why did these events happen?
                                                                                    Why did the people act this way?

Does this verse reveal anything about God/Jesus/Holy Spirit?
Are there examples to follow or avoid? What does this chapter have to teach me?

How can I apply insights from this verse today? This week?

Notes, quotes, doodles, checklists, prayers, etc.

#Iwillmeditate

Numbers 31

Date:

Summarize the main idea(s) in this chapter:

Verse(s) that stood out   or   Who is in this chapter?
What do they say? What do they do?

Why did I pick this verse?   or   What is going on?
Is there anything going wrong?

Definitions of words and/or   or   When and where
cross references from my verse   did this happen?

Rewrite the verse in your own words   or   Why is this chapter in the Bible?
or personalize it.   Why did these events happen?
                                                                               Why did the people act this way?

Does this verse reveal anything about God/Jesus/Holy Spirit?
Are there examples to follow or avoid? What does this chapter have to teach me?

How can I apply insights from this verse today? This week?

Notes, quotes, doodles, checklists, prayers, etc.

#Iwillmeditate

Numbers 32

Date:

Summarize the main idea(s) in this chapter:

Verse(s) that stood out   or   Who is in this chapter?
What do they say? What do they do?

Why did I pick this verse?   or   What is going on?
Is there anything going wrong?

Definitions of words and/or   or   When and where
cross references from my verse   did this happen?

Rewrite the verse in your own words   or   Why is this chapter in the Bible?
or personalize it.   Why did these events happen?
                                                                              Why did the people act this way?

Does this verse reveal anything about God/Jesus/Holy Spirit?
Are there examples to follow or avoid? What does this chapter have to teach me?

How can I apply insights from this verse today? This week?

Notes, quotes, doodles, checklists, prayers, etc.

#Iwillmeditate

Numbers 33

Date:

Summarize the main idea(s) in this chapter:

Verse(s) that stood out   or   Who is in this chapter?
What do they say? What do they do?

Why did I pick this verse?   or   What is going on?
Is there anything going wrong?

Definitions of words and/or   or   When and where
cross references from my verse   did this happen?

Rewrite the verse in your own words or personalize it.

or

Why is this chapter in the Bible?
Why did these events happen?
Why did the people act this way?

Does this verse reveal anything about God/Jesus/Holy Spirit?
Are there examples to follow or avoid? What does this chapter have to teach me?

How can I apply insights from this verse today? This week?

Notes, quotes, doodles, checklists, prayers, etc.

Review and reflect #33

Date:

Review each of the last six days work. Write or list the main takeaway you got from each chapter. (Look closely at the sections "What does this reveal about God?" and "How can I apply this?")

Are there any themes showing up in this week's work?

Are there any areas God is wanting to grow my faith or trust?
Are there any insights from this week's work on how to do this?

Are there any sins God is spotlighting in my life?
Are there any insights from this week's work on how to kill these sins?

Re-read one or two of the most impactful verses from this week and turn them into a prayer. (There is room on the next pages to write it down if you want.)

How can I thank or praise God as a result of what I've learned this week?

How can I apply what I've learned this week to my life today and next week?

Where do I need His strength for today? Tomorrow? Next week?

Is there a verse from this week that I should commit to memory? Write it on the next page or on a 3x5 card to take with you to memorize.

Are there any sins I need to confess to God in prayer?

Is there anyone I need to forgive? Is there anyone I need to ask forgiveness of?

Are there any seeds of bitterness starting to take root in my heart?

Are there any fears or worries I need to lay at His feet?

#Iwillmeditate

notes, verses to memorize

prayers, doodles, etc

Numbers 34

Date:

Summarize the main idea(s) in this chapter:

Verse(s) that stood out   or   Who is in this chapter?
What do they say? What do they do?

Why did I pick this verse?   or   What is going on?
Is there anything going wrong?

Definitions of words and/or   or   When and where
cross references from my verse   did this happen?

Rewrite the verse in your own words or personalize it.   or   Why is this chapter in the Bible? Why did these events happen? Why did the people act this way?

Does this verse reveal anything about God/Jesus/Holy Spirit? Are there examples to follow or avoid? What does this chapter have to teach me?

How can I apply insights from this verse today? This week?

Notes, quotes, doodles, checklists, prayers, etc.

#Iwillmeditate

Numbers 35

Date:

Summarize the main idea(s) in this chapter:

Verse(s) that stood out   or   Who is in this chapter?
What do they say? What do they do?

Why did I pick this verse?   or   What is going on?
Is there anything going wrong?

Definitions of words and/or   or   When and where
cross references from my verse   did this happen?

Rewrite the verse in your own words or personalize it.   or   Why is this chapter in the Bible?
                                                                                  Why did these events happen?
                                                                                  Why did the people act this way?

Does this verse reveal anything about God/Jesus/Holy Spirit?
Are there examples to follow or avoid? What does this chapter have to teach me?

How can I apply insights from this verse today? This week?

Notes, quotes, doodles, checklists, prayers, etc.

Numbers 36

Date:

Summarize the main idea(s) in this chapter:

Verse(s) that stood out   or   Who is in this chapter?
What do they say? What do they do?

Why did I pick this verse?   or   What is going on?
Is there anything going wrong?

Definitions of words and/or   or   When and where
cross references from my verse   did this happen?

Rewrite the verse in your own words   or   Why is this chapter in the Bible?
or personalize it.   Why did these events happen?
                                                                               Why did the people act this way?

Does this verse reveal anything about God/Jesus/Holy Spirit?
Are there examples to follow or avoid? What does this chapter have to teach me?

How can I apply insights from this verse today? This week?

Notes, quotes, doodles, checklists, prayers, etc.

#Iwillmeditate

The Gospel of John

Jesus God Father world come know answered man Gospel of John Jews one things came disciples believe life sent went may Son Now heard Lord people away going also Pharisees Simon Peter Christ witness love another saw given see truth water judge place sheep believed Truly receive

the book of John preview

Take some time to learn about the book of John and where it fits into the overall narrative of the Bible, and key themes to look for.

At the beginning of each new book of the Bible, I've included two preview pages for you to use to journal and take notes.

- Read the introduction in your Bible.

- Visit TheBibleProject.com. I highly recommend creating an account (it's free). All their information on numbers is here: https://thebibleproject.com/explore/numbers/

- If you want to go even further, there are great free introductions to the book of numbers online. Here are some I love:

- From Grace to You:
https://www.gty.org/library/bible-introductions

- From Precept Austin:
http://www.preceptaustin.org/bybook

- Blue Letter Bible:
https://www.blueletterbible.org/resources/intros.cfm

the book of John notes

Palestine in the Time of Jesus, A.D. 6 to 30

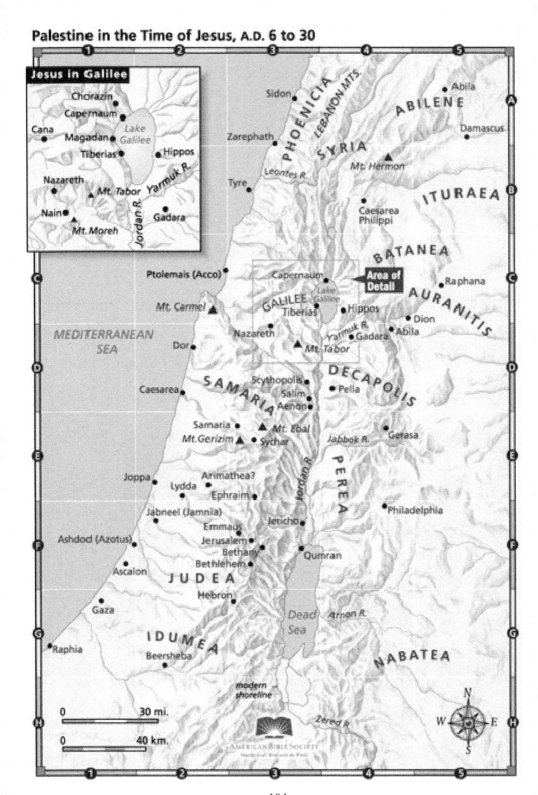

Jesus in Galilee

Chorazin
Capernaum
Cana
Lake Galilee
Magadan
Tiberias
Hippos
Nazareth
Mt. Tabor
Yarmuk R.
Nain
Jordan R.
Mt. Moreh
Gadara

Sidon
Abila
PHOENICIA
LEBANON MTS.
ABILENE
Damascus
Zarephath
SYRIA
Tyre
Leontes R.
Mt. Hermon
ITURAEA
Caesarea Philippi
BATANEA
Ptolemais (Acco)
Capernaum
Area of Detail
Raphana
AURANITIS
Mt. Carmel
GALILEE
Lake Galilee
Hippos
Dion
MEDITERRANEAN SEA
Tiberias
Yarmuk R.
Abila
Dor
Nazareth
Gadara
Mt. Tabor
DECAPOLIS
Caesarea
Scythopolis
Pella
SAMARIA
Salim
Aenon
Samaria
Mt. Ebal
Gerasa
Mt. Gerizim
Sychar
Jabbok R.
Joppa
Arimathea?
Lydda
Ephraim
PEREA
Jabneel (Jamnia)
Jericho
Philadelphia
Emmaus
Ashdod (Azotus)
Jerusalem
Bethany
Qumran
Bethlehem
JUDEA
Hebron
Ascalon
Gaza
Dead Sea
Arnon R.
IDUMEA
Raphia
Beersheba
NABATEA
modern shoreline
Zered R.

0 ___ 30 mi.
0 ___ 40 km.

AMERICAN BIBLE SOCIETY

N W E S

Jerusalem in the Time of Jesus, Around A.D. 30

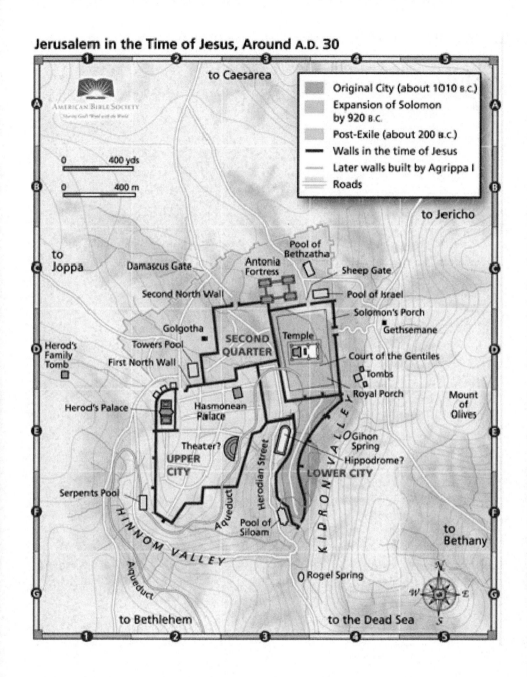

These maps are in the public domain. They were published in 1888 by the American Bible Society. Feel free to take photocopies and highlight where Jesus was as you read through John. I tape them into my meditation notes for the chapter.

John 1

Date:

Summarize the main idea(s) in this chapter:

Verse(s) that stood out   or   Who is in this chapter?
What do they say? What do they do?

Why did I pick this verse?   or   What is going on?
Is there anything going wrong?

Definitions of words and/or   or   When and where
cross references from my verse   did this happen?

Rewrite the verse in your own words   or   Why is this chapter in the Bible?
or personalize it.   Why did these events happen?
                                                                        Why did the people act this way?

Does this verse reveal anything about God/Jesus/Holy Spirit?
Are there examples to follow or avoid? What does this chapter have to teach me?

How can I apply insights from this verse today? This week?

Notes, quotes, doodles, checklists, prayers, etc.

#Iwillmeditate

John 2

Date:

Summarize the main idea(s) in this chapter:

Verse(s) that stood out   or   Who is in this chapter?
What do they say? What do they do?

Why did I pick this verse?   or   What is going on?
Is there anything going wrong?

Definitions of words and/or   or   When and where
cross references from my verse   did this happen?

Rewrite the verse in your own words   or   Why is this chapter in the Bible?
or personalize it.   Why did these events happen?
                                                                                  Why did the people act this way?

Does this verse reveal anything about God/Jesus/Holy Spirit?
Are there examples to follow or avoid? What does this chapter have to teach me?

How can I apply insights from this verse today? This week?

Notes, quotes, doodles, checklists, prayers, etc.

#Iwillmeditate

John 3

Date:

Summarize the main idea(s) in this chapter:

Verse(s) that stood out   or   Who is in this chapter?
What do they say? What do they do?

Why did I pick this verse?   or   What is going on?
Is there anything going wrong?

Definitions of words and/or   or   When and where
cross references from my verse   did this happen?

Rewrite the verse in your own words   or   Why is this chapter in the Bible?
or personalize it.   Why did these events happen?
                                                     Why did the people act this way?

Does this verse reveal anything about God/Jesus/Holy Spirit?
Are there examples to follow or avoid? What does this chapter have to teach me?

How can I apply insights from this verse today? This week?

Notes, quotes, doodles, checklists, prayers, etc.

Review and reflect #34

Date:

Review each of the last six days work. Write or list the main takeaway you got from each chapter. (Look closely at the sections "What does this reveal about God?" and "How can I apply this?")

Are there any themes showing up in this week's work?

Are there any areas God is wanting to grow my faith or trust?
Are there any insights from this week's work on how to do this?

Are there any sins God is spotlighting in my life?
Are there any insights from this week's work on how to kill these sins?

Re-read one or two of the most impactful verses from this week and turn them into a prayer. (There is room on the next pages to write it down if you want.)

How can I thank or praise God as a result of what I've learned this week?

How can I apply what I've learned this week to my life today and next week?

Where do I need His strength for today? Tomorrow? Next week?

Is there a verse from this week that I should commit to memory? Write it on the next page or on a 3x5 card to take with you to memorize.

Are there any sins I need to confess to God in prayer?

Is there anyone I need to forgive? Is there anyone I need to ask forgiveness of?

Are there any seeds of bitterness starting to take root in my heart?

Are there any fears or worries I need to lay at His feet?

#Iwillmeditate

notes, verses to memorize

prayers, doodles, etc

John 4

Date:

Summarize the main idea(s) in this chapter:

Verse(s) that stood out   or   Who is in this chapter?
What do they say? What do they do?

Why did I pick this verse?   or   What is going on?
Is there anything going wrong?

Definitions of words and/or   or   When and where
cross references from my verse   did this happen?

Rewrite the verse in your own words   or   Why is this chapter in the Bible?
or personalize it.   Why did these events happen?
    Why did the people act this way?

Does this verse reveal anything about God/Jesus/Holy Spirit?
Are there examples to follow or avoid? What does this chapter have to teach me?

How can I apply insights from this verse today? This week?

Notes, quotes, doodles, checklists, prayers, etc.

#Iwillmeditate

John 5

Date:

Summarize the main idea(s) in this chapter:

Verse(s) that stood out   or   Who is in this chapter?
What do they say? What do they do?

Why did I pick this verse?   or   What is going on?
Is there anything going wrong?

Definitions of words and/or   or   When and where
cross references from my verse   did this happen?

Rewrite the verse in your own words
or personalize it.

or

Why is this chapter in the Bible?
Why did these events happen?
Why did the people act this way?

Does this verse reveal anything about God/Jesus/Holy Spirit?
Are there examples to follow or avoid? What does this chapter have to teach me?

How can I apply insights from this verse today? This week?

Notes, quotes, doodles, checklists, prayers, etc.

#Iwillmeditate

John 6

Date:

Summarize the main idea(s) in this chapter:

Verse(s) that stood out   or   Who is in this chapter?
What do they say? What do they do?

Why did I pick this verse?   or   What is going on?
Is there anything going wrong?

Definitions of words and/or   or   When and where
cross references from my verse   did this happen?

Rewrite the verse in your own words   or   Why is this chapter in the Bible?
or personalize it.

Why did these events happen?

Why did the people act this way?

Does this verse reveal anything about God/Jesus/Holy Spirit?
Are there examples to follow or avoid? What does this chapter have to teach me?

How can I apply insights from this verse today? This week?

Notes, quotes, doodles, checklists, prayers, etc.

John 7

Date:

Summarize the main idea(s) in this chapter:

Verse(s) that stood out   or   Who is in this chapter?
What do they say? What do they do?

Why did I pick this verse?   or   What is going on?
Is there anything going wrong?

Definitions of words and/or   or   When and where
cross references from my verse   did this happen?

Rewrite the verse in your own words or Why is this chapter in the Bible?
or personalize it. Why did these events happen?
Why did the people act this way?

Does this verse reveal anything about God/Jesus/Holy Spirit?
Are there examples to follow or avoid? What does this chapter have to teach me?

How can I apply insights from this verse today? This week?

Notes, quotes, doodles, checklists, prayers, etc.

#Iwillmeditate

John 8

Date:

Summarize the main idea(s) in this chapter:

Verse(s) that stood out   or   Who is in this chapter?
What do they say? What do they do?

Why did I pick this verse?   or   What is going on?
Is there anything going wrong?

Definitions of words and/or   or   When and where
cross references from my verse   did this happen?

Rewrite the verse in your own words or personalize it.

or

Why is this chapter in the Bible?
Why did these events happen?
Why did the people act this way?

Does this verse reveal anything about God/Jesus/Holy Spirit?
Are there examples to follow or avoid? What does this chapter have to teach me?

How can I apply insights from this verse today? This week?

Notes, quotes, doodles, checklists, prayers, etc.

#Iwillmeditate

John 9

Date:

Summarize the main idea(s) in this chapter:

Verse(s) that stood out   or   Who is in this chapter?
What do they say? What do they do?

Why did I pick this verse?   or   What is going on?
Is there anything going wrong?

Definitions of words and/or   or   When and where
cross references from my verse   did this happen?

Rewrite the verse in your own words or personalize it.

or

Why is this chapter in the Bible?
Why did these events happen?
Why did the people act this way?

Does this verse reveal anything about God/Jesus/Holy Spirit?
Are there examples to follow or avoid? What does this chapter have to teach me?

How can I apply insights from this verse today? This week?

Notes, quotes, doodles, checklists, prayers, etc.

#Iwillmeditate

Review and reflect #34

Date:

Review each of the last six days work. Write or list the main takeaway you got from each chapter. (Look closely at the sections "What does this reveal about God?" and "How can I apply this?")

Are there any themes showing up in this week's work?

Are there any areas God is wanting to grow my faith or trust?
Are there any insights from this week's work on how to do this?

Are there any sins God is spotlighting in my life?
Are there any insights from this week's work on how to kill these sins?

Re-read one or two of the most impactful verses from this week and turn them into a prayer. (There is room on the next pages to write it down if you want.)

How can I thank or praise God as a result of what I've learned this week?

How can I apply what I've learned this week to my life today and next week?

Where do I need His strength for today? Tomorrow? Next week?

Is there a verse from this week that I should commit to memory? Write it on the next page or on a 3x5 card to take with you to memorize.

Are there any sins I need to confess to God in prayer?

Is there anyone I need to forgive? Is there anyone I need to ask forgiveness of?

Are there any seeds of bitterness starting to take root in my heart?

Are there any fears or worries I need to lay at His feet?

#Iwillmeditate

notes, verses to memorize

prayers, doodles, etc

John 10

Date:

Summarize the main idea(s) in this chapter:

Verse(s) that stood out   or   Who is in this chapter?
What do they say? What do they do?

Why did I pick this verse?   or   What is going on?
Is there anything going wrong?

Definitions of words and/or   or   When and where
cross references from my verse   did this happen?

Rewrite the verse in your own words or personalize it.

or

Why is this chapter in the Bible?
Why did these events happen?
Why did the people act this way?

Does this verse reveal anything about God/Jesus/Holy Spirit?
Are there examples to follow or avoid? What does this chapter have to teach me?

How can I apply insights from this verse today? This week?

Notes, quotes, doodles, checklists, prayers, etc.

#Iwillmeditate

John 11

Date:

Summarize the main idea(s) in this chapter:

Verse(s) that stood out   or   Who is in this chapter?
What do they say? What do they do?

Why did I pick this verse?   or   What is going on?
Is there anything going wrong?

Definitions of words and/or   or   When and where
cross references from my verse   did this happen?

Rewrite the verse in your own words   or   Why is this chapter in the Bible?
or personalize it.   Why did these events happen?
                                                                          Why did the people act this way?

Does this verse reveal anything about God/Jesus/Holy Spirit?
Are there examples to follow or avoid? What does this chapter have to teach me?

How can I apply insights from this verse today? This week?

Notes, quotes, doodles, checklists, prayers, etc.

#Iwillmeditate

John 12

Date:

Summarize the main idea(s) in this chapter:

Verse(s) that stood out   or   Who is in this chapter?
What do they say? What do they do?

Why did I pick this verse?   or   What is going on?
Is there anything going wrong?

Definitions of words and/or   or   When and where
cross references from my verse   did this happen?

Rewrite the verse in your own words or personalize it.   or   Why is this chapter in the Bible?
Why did these events happen?
Why did the people act this way?

Does this verse reveal anything about God/Jesus/Holy Spirit?
Are there examples to follow or avoid? What does this chapter have to teach me?

How can I apply insights from this verse today? This week?

Notes, quotes, doodles, checklists, prayers, etc.

#Iwillmeditate

John 13

Date:

Summarize the main idea(s) in this chapter:

Verse(s) that stood out   or   Who is in this chapter?
What do they say? What do they do?

Why did I pick this verse?   or   What is going on?
Is there anything going wrong?

Definitions of words and/or   or   When and where
cross references from my verse   did this happen?

Rewrite the verse in your own words   or   Why is this chapter in the Bible?
or personalize it.   Why did these events happen?
                                                                     Why did the people act this way?

Does this verse reveal anything about God/Jesus/Holy Spirit?
Are there examples to follow or avoid? What does this chapter have to teach me?

How can I apply insights from this verse today? This week?

Notes, quotes, doodles, checklists, prayers, etc.

#Iwillmeditate

John 14

Date:

Summarize the main idea(s) in this chapter:

Verse(s) that stood out   or   Who is in this chapter?
What do they say? What do they do?

Why did I pick this verse?   or   What is going on?
Is there anything going wrong?

Definitions of words and/or   or   When and where
cross references from my verse   did this happen?

Rewrite the verse in your own words
or personalize it.

or

Why is this chapter in the Bible?
Why did these events happen?
Why did the people act this way?

Does this verse reveal anything about God/Jesus/Holy Spirit?
Are there examples to follow or avoid? What does this chapter have to teach me?

How can I apply insights from this verse today? This week?

Notes, quotes, doodles, checklists, prayers, etc.

#Iwillmeditate

John 15

Date:

Summarize the main idea(s) in this chapter:

Verse(s) that stood out   or   Who is in this chapter?
                                              What do they say? What do they do?

Why did I pick this verse?   or   What is going on?
                                                Is there anything going wrong?

Definitions of words and/or   or   When and where
cross references from my verse   did this happen?

Rewrite the verse in your own words or personalize it.   or   Why is this chapter in the Bible? Why did these events happen? Why did the people act this way?

Does this verse reveal anything about God/Jesus/Holy Spirit?
Are there examples to follow or avoid? What does this chapter have to teach me?

How can I apply insights from this verse today? This week?

Notes, quotes, doodles, checklists, prayers, etc.

Review and reflect #35

Date:

Review each of the last six days work. Write or list the main takeaway you got from each chapter. (Look closely at the sections "What does this reveal about God?" and "How can I apply this?")

Are there any themes showing up in this week's work?

Are there any areas God is wanting to grow my faith or trust?
Are there any insights from this week's work on how to do this?

Are there any sins God is spotlighting in my life?
Are there any insights from this week's work on how to kill these sins?

Re-read one or two of the most impactful verses from this week and turn them into a prayer. (There is room on the next pages to write it down if you want.)

How can I thank or praise God as a result of what I've learned this week?

How can I apply what I've learned this week to my life today and next week?

Where do I need His strength for today? Tomorrow? Next week?

Is there a verse from this week that I should commit to memory? Write it on the next page or on a 3x5 card to take with you to memorize.

Are there any sins I need to confess to God in prayer?

Is there anyone I need to forgive? Is there anyone I need to ask forgiveness of?

Are there any seeds of bitterness starting to take root in my heart?

Are there any fears or worries I need to lay at His feet?

#Iwillmeditate

notes, verses to memorize

prayers, doodles, etc

John 16

Date:

Summarize the main idea(s) in this chapter:

Verse(s) that stood out   or   Who is in this chapter?
What do they say? What do they do?

Why did I pick this verse?   or   What is going on?
Is there anything going wrong?

Definitions of words and/or   or   When and where
cross references from my verse   did this happen?

Rewrite the verse in your own words
or personalize it.

or

Why is this chapter in the Bible?
Why did these events happen?
Why did the people act this way?

Does this verse reveal anything about God/Jesus/Holy Spirit?
Are there examples to follow or avoid? What does this chapter have to teach me?

How can I apply insights from this verse today? This week?

Notes, quotes, doodles, checklists, prayers, etc.

#Iwillmeditate

John 17

Date:

Summarize the main idea(s) in this chapter:

Verse(s) that stood out   or   Who is in this chapter?
What do they say? What do they do?

Why did I pick this verse?   or   What is going on?
Is there anything going wrong?

Definitions of words and/or   or   When and where
cross references from my verse   did this happen?

Rewrite the verse in your own words or personalize it.

or

Why is this chapter in the Bible?
Why did these events happen?
Why did the people act this way?

Does this verse reveal anything about God/Jesus/Holy Spirit?
Are there examples to follow or avoid? What does this chapter have to teach me?

How can I apply insights from this verse today? This week?

Notes, quotes, doodles, checklists, prayers, etc.

#Iwillmeditate

John 18

Date:

Summarize the main idea(s) in this chapter:

Verse(s) that stood out   or   Who is in this chapter?
What do they say? What do they do?

Why did I pick this verse?   or   What is going on?
Is there anything going wrong?

Definitions of words and/or   or   When and where
cross references from my verse   did this happen?

Rewrite the verse in your own words   or   Why is this chapter in the Bible?
or personalize it.   Why did these events happen?
                                                                                   Why did the people act this way?

Does this verse reveal anything about God/Jesus/Holy Spirit?
Are there examples to follow or avoid? What does this chapter have to teach me?

How can I apply insights from this verse today? This week?

Notes, quotes, doodles, checklists, prayers, etc.

#Iwillmeditate

John 19

Date:

Summarize the main idea(s) in this chapter:

Verse(s) that stood out   or   Who is in this chapter?
What do they say? What do they do?

Why did I pick this verse?   or   What is going on?
Is there anything going wrong?

Definitions of words and/or   or   When and where
cross references from my verse   did this happen?

Rewrite the verse in your own words
or personalize it.

or

Why is this chapter in the Bible?
Why did these events happen?
Why did the people act this way?

Does this verse reveal anything about God/Jesus/Holy Spirit?
Are there examples to follow or avoid? What does this chapter have to teach me?

How can I apply insights from this verse today? This week?

Notes, quotes, doodles, checklists, prayers, etc.

#Iwillmeditate

John 20

Date:

Summarize the main idea(s) in this chapter:

Verse(s) that stood out   or   Who is in this chapter?
What do they say? What do they do?

Why did I pick this verse?   or   What is going on?
Is there anything going wrong?

Definitions of words and/or   or   When and where
cross references from my verse   did this happen?

Rewrite the verse in your own words   or   Why is this chapter in the Bible?
or personalize it.   Why did these events happen?
                                                                             Why did the people act this way?

Does this verse reveal anything about God/Jesus/Holy Spirit?
Are there examples to follow or avoid? What does this chapter have to teach me?

How can I apply insights from this verse today? This week?

Notes, quotes, doodles, checklists, prayers, etc.

#Iwillmeditate

John 21

Date:

Summarize the main idea(s) in this chapter:

Verse(s) that stood out   or   Who is in this chapter?
What do they say? What do they do?

Why did I pick this verse?   or   What is going on?
Is there anything going wrong?

Definitions of words and/or   or   When and where
cross references from my verse   did this happen?

Rewrite the verse in your own words   or   Why is this chapter in the Bible?
or personalize it.   Why did these events happen?
                                                                        Why did the people act this way?

Does this verse reveal anything about God/Jesus/Holy Spirit?
Are there examples to follow or avoid? What does this chapter have to teach me?

How can I apply insights from this verse today? This week?

Notes, quotes, doodles, checklists, prayers, etc.

#Iwillmeditate

Review and reflect #36

Date:

Review each of the last six days work. Write or list the main takeaway you got from each chapter. (Look closely at the sections "What does this reveal about God?" and "How can I apply this?")

Are there any themes showing up in this week's work?

Are there any areas God is wanting to grow my faith or trust?
Are there any insights from this week's work on how to do this?

Are there any sins God is spotlighting in my life?
Are there any insights from this week's work on how to kill these sins?

Re-read one or two of the most impactful verses from this week and turn them into a prayer. (There is room on the next pages to write it down if you want.)

How can I thank or praise God as a result of what I've learned this week?

How can I apply what I've learned this week to my life today and next week?

Where do I need His strength for today? Tomorrow? Next week?

Is there a verse from this week that I should commit to memory? Write it on the next page or on a 3x5 card to take with you to memorize.

Are there any sins I need to confess to God in prayer?

Is there anyone I need to forgive? Is there anyone I need to ask forgiveness of?

Are there any seeds of bitterness starting to take root in my heart?

Are there any fears or worries I need to lay at His feet?

#Iwillmeditate

notes, verses to memorize

prayers, doodles, etc

Image courtesy of Blue Letter Bible. Used with permission.

the book of Deuteronomy preview

Take some time to learn about the book of Deuteronomy, where it fits into the overall narrative of the Bible, key themes, and things to watch for. Use these preview pages to take notes.

- Read the introduction in your Bible.

- Visit TheBibleProject.com. I highly recommend creating an account (it's free). All their information on numbers is here: https://thebibleproject.com/explore/numbers/

- If you want to go even further, there are great free introductions to the book of numbers online. Here are some I love:

- From Grace to You: https://www.gty.org/library/bible-introductions

- From Precept Austin: http://www.preceptaustin.org/bybook

- Blue Letter Bible: https://www.blueletterbible.org/resources/intros.cfm

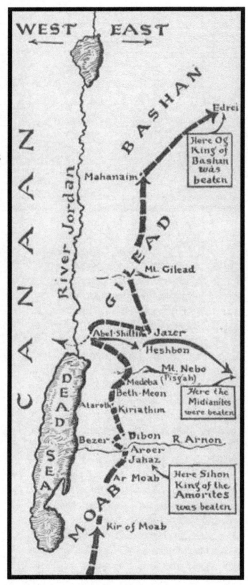

the book of Deuteronomy notes

Deuteronomy 1

Date:

Summarize the main idea(s) in this chapter:

Verse(s) that stood out   or   Who is in this chapter?
What do they say? What do they do?

Why did I pick this verse?   or   What is going on?
Is there anything going wrong?

Definitions of words and/or   or   When and where
cross references from my verse   did this happen?

Rewrite the verse in your own words   or   Why is this chapter in the Bible?
or personalize it.   Why did these events happen?
                                                                Why did the people act this way?

Does this verse reveal anything about God/Jesus/Holy Spirit?
Are there examples to follow or avoid? What does this chapter have to teach me?

How can I apply insights from this verse today? This week?

Notes, quotes, doodles, checklists, prayers, etc.

#Iwillmeditate

Deuteronomy 2

Date:

Summarize the main idea(s) in this chapter:

Verse(s) that stood out   or   Who is in this chapter?
What do they say? What do they do?

Why did I pick this verse?   or   What is going on?
Is there anything going wrong?

Definitions of words and/or   or   When and where
cross references from my verse   did this happen?

Rewrite the verse in your own words   or   Why is this chapter in the Bible?
or personalize it.   Why did these events happen?
                                                            Why did the people act this way?

Does this verse reveal anything about God/Jesus/Holy Spirit?
Are there examples to follow or avoid? What does this chapter have to teach me?

How can I apply insights from this verse today? This week?

Notes, quotes, doodles, checklists, prayers, etc.

#Iwillmeditate

Deuteronomy 3

Date:

Summarize the main idea(s) in this chapter:

Verse(s) that stood out   or   Who is in this chapter?
What do they say? What do they do?

Why did I pick this verse?   or   What is going on?
Is there anything going wrong?

Definitions of words and/or   or   When and where
cross references from my verse   did this happen?

Rewrite the verse in your own words   or   Why is this chapter in the Bible?
or personalize it.   Why did these events happen?
                                                                      Why did the people act this way?

Does this verse reveal anything about God/Jesus/Holy Spirit?
Are there examples to follow or avoid? What does this chapter have to teach me?

How can I apply insights from this verse today? This week?

Notes, quotes, doodles, checklists, prayers, etc.

#Iwillmeditate

Deuteronomy 4

Date:

Summarize the main idea(s) in this chapter:

Verse(s) that stood out   or   Who is in this chapter?
What do they say? What do they do?

Why did I pick this verse?   or   What is going on?
Is there anything going wrong?

Definitions of words and/or   or   When and where
cross references from my verse   did this happen?

Rewrite the verse in your own words or personalize it.   or   Why is this chapter in the Bible?
                                                                                     Why did these events happen?
                                                                                     Why did the people act this way?

Does this verse reveal anything about God/Jesus/Holy Spirit?
Are there examples to follow or avoid? What does this chapter have to teach me?

How can I apply insights from this verse today? This week?

Notes, quotes, doodles, checklists, prayers, etc.

#Iwillmeditate

Deuteronomy 5

Date:

Summarize the main idea(s) in this chapter:

Verse(s) that stood out   or   Who is in this chapter?
What do they say? What do they do?

Why did I pick this verse?   or   What is going on?
Is there anything going wrong?

Definitions of words and/or   or   When and where
cross references from my verse   did this happen?

Rewrite the verse in your own words   or   Why is this chapter in the Bible?
or personalize it.   Why did these events happen?
                                                              Why did the people act this way?

Does this verse reveal anything about God/Jesus/Holy Spirit?
Are there examples to follow or avoid? What does this chapter have to teach me?

How can I apply insights from this verse today? This week?

Notes, quotes, doodles, checklists, prayers, etc.

Deuteronomy 6-7

Date:

Summarize the main idea(s) in this chapter:

Verse(s) that stood out   or   Who is in this chapter?
What do they say? What do they do?

Why did I pick this verse?   or   What is going on?
Is there anything going wrong?

Definitions of words and/or   or   When and where
cross references from my verse   did this happen?

Rewrite the verse in your own words   or   Why is this chapter in the Bible?
or personalize it.   Why did these events happen?
                                                            Why did the people act this way?

Does this verse reveal anything about God/Jesus/Holy Spirit?
Are there examples to follow or avoid? What does this chapter have to teach me?

How can I apply insights from this verse today? This week?

Notes, quotes, doodles, checklists, prayers, etc.

#Iwillmeditate

Review and reflect #37

Date:

Review each of the last six days work. Write or list the main takeaway you got from each chapter. (Look closely at the sections "What does this reveal about God?" and "How can I apply this?")

Are there any themes showing up in this week's work?

Are there any areas God is wanting to grow my faith or trust?
Are there any insights from this week's work on how to do this?

Are there any sins God is spotlighting in my life?
Are there any insights from this week's work on how to kill these sins?

Re-read one or two of the most impactful verses from this week and turn them into a prayer. (There is room on the next pages to write it down if you want.)

How can I thank or praise God as a result of what I've learned this week?

How can I apply what I've learned this week to my life today and next week?

Where do I need His strength for today? Tomorrow? Next week?

Is there a verse from this week that I should commit to memory? Write it on the next page or on a 3x5 card to take with you to memorize.

Are there any sins I need to confess to God in prayer?

Is there anyone I need to forgive? Is there anyone I need to ask forgiveness of?

Are there any seeds of bitterness starting to take root in my heart?

Are there any fears or worries I need to lay at His feet?

notes, verses to memorize

prayers, doodles, etc

Deuteronomy 8-9

Date:

Summarize the main idea(s) in this chapter:

Verse(s) that stood out   or   Who is in this chapter?
What do they say? What do they do?

Why did I pick this verse?   or   What is going on?
Is there anything going wrong?

Definitions of words and/or   or   When and where
cross references from my verse   did this happen?

Rewrite the verse in your own words or personalize it.

or

Why is this chapter in the Bible?
Why did these events happen?
Why did the people act this way?

Does this verse reveal anything about God/Jesus/Holy Spirit?
Are there examples to follow or avoid? What does this chapter have to teach me?

How can I apply insights from this verse today? This week?

Notes, quotes, doodles, checklists, prayers, etc.

#Iwillmeditate

Deuteronomy 10

Date:

Summarize the main idea(s) in this chapter:

Verse(s) that stood out | or | Who is in this chapter?
What do they say? What do they do?

Why did I pick this verse? | or | What is going on?
Is there anything going wrong?

Definitions of words and/or | or | When and where
cross references from my verse | | did this happen?

Rewrite the verse in your own words   or   Why is this chapter in the Bible?
or personalize it.   Why did these events happen?
                                                                             Why did the people act this way?

Does this verse reveal anything about God/Jesus/Holy Spirit?
Are there examples to follow or avoid? What does this chapter have to teach me?

How can I apply insights from this verse today? This week?

Notes, quotes, doodles, checklists, prayers, etc.

#Iwillmeditate

Deuteronomy 11

Date:

Summarize the main idea(s) in this chapter:

Verse(s) that stood out   or   Who is in this chapter?
                                              What do they say? What do they do?

Why did I pick this verse?   or   What is going on?
                                                 Is there anything going wrong?

Definitions of words and/or   or   When and where
cross references from my verse   did this happen?

Rewrite the verse in your own words or personalize it.

or

Why is this chapter in the Bible?
Why did these events happen?
Why did the people act this way?

Does this verse reveal anything about God/Jesus/Holy Spirit?
Are there examples to follow or avoid? What does this chapter have to teach me?

How can I apply insights from this verse today? This week?

Notes, quotes, doodles, checklists, prayers, etc.

#Iwillmeditate

Deuteronomy 12

Date:

Summarize the main idea(s) in this chapter:

Verse(s) that stood out   or   Who is in this chapter?
What do they say? What do they do?

Why did I pick this verse?   or   What is going on?
Is there anything going wrong?

Definitions of words and/or   or   When and where
cross references from my verse   did this happen?

Rewrite the verse in your own words   or   Why is this chapter in the Bible?
or personalize it.   Why did these events happen?
                                                Why did the people act this way?

Does this verse reveal anything about God/Jesus/Holy Spirit?
Are there examples to follow or avoid? What does this chapter have to teach me?

How can I apply insights from this verse today? This week?

Notes, quotes, doodles, checklists, prayers, etc.

#Iwillmeditate

Deuteronomy 13-14

Date:

Summarize the main idea(s) in this chapter:

Verse(s) that stood out   or   Who is in this chapter?
What do they say? What do they do?

Why did I pick this verse?   or   What is going on?
Is there anything going wrong?

Definitions of words and/or   or   When and where
cross references from my verse   did this happen?

Rewrite the verse in your own words or personalize it.

or

Why is this chapter in the Bible?
Why did these events happen?
Why did the people act this way?

Does this verse reveal anything about God/Jesus/Holy Spirit?
Are there examples to follow or avoid? What does this chapter have to teach me?

How can I apply insights from this verse today? This week?

Notes, quotes, doodles, checklists, prayers, etc.

#Iwillmeditate

Deuteronomy 15-16

Date:

Summarize the main idea(s) in this chapter:

Verse(s) that stood out   or   Who is in this chapter?
What do they say? What do they do?

Why did I pick this verse?   or   What is going on?
Is there anything going wrong?

Definitions of words and/or   or   When and where
cross references from my verse   did this happen?

Rewrite the verse in your own words   or   Why is this chapter in the Bible?
or personalize it.   Why did these events happen?
                                                                Why did the people act this way?

Does this verse reveal anything about God/Jesus/Holy Spirit?
Are there examples to follow or avoid? What does this chapter have to teach me?

How can I apply insights from this verse today? This week?

Notes, quotes, doodles, checklists, prayers, etc.

#Iwillmeditate

Review and reflect #38

Date:

Review each of the last six days work. Write or list the main takeaway you got from each chapter. (Look closely at the sections "What does this reveal about God?" and "How can I apply this?")

Are there any themes showing up in this week's work?

Are there any areas God is wanting to grow my faith or trust?
Are there any insights from this week's work on how to do this?

Are there any sins God is spotlighting in my life?
Are there any insights from this week's work on how to kill these sins?

Re-read one or two of the most impactful verses from this week and turn them into a prayer. (There is room on the next pages to write it down if you want.)

How can I thank or praise God as a result of what I've learned this week?

How can I apply what I've learned this week to my life today and next week?

Where do I need His strength for today? Tomorrow? Next week?

Is there a verse from this week that I should commit to memory? Write it on the next page or on a 3x5 card to take with you to memorize.

Are there any sins I need to confess to God in prayer?

Is there anyone I need to forgive? Is there anyone I need to ask forgiveness of?

Are there any seeds of bitterness starting to take root in my heart?

Are there any fears or worries I need to lay at His feet?

#Iwillmeditate

notes, verses to memorize

prayers, doodles, etc

Deuteronomy 17-18

Date:

Summarize the main idea(s) in this chapter:

Verse(s) that stood out   or   Who is in this chapter?
What do they say? What do they do?

Why did I pick this verse?   or   What is going on?
Is there anything going wrong?

Definitions of words and/or   or   When and where
cross references from my verse   did this happen?

Rewrite the verse in your own words   or   Why is this chapter in the Bible?
or personalize it.   Why did these events happen?
                                                                     Why did the people act this way?

Does this verse reveal anything about God/Jesus/Holy Spirit?
Are there examples to follow or avoid? What does this chapter have to teach me?

How can I apply insights from this verse today? This week?

Notes, quotes, doodles, checklists, prayers, etc.

#Iwillmeditate

Deuteronomy 19-20

Date:

Summarize the main idea(s) in this chapter:

Verse(s) that stood out   or   Who is in this chapter?
What do they say? What do they do?

Why did I pick this verse?   or   What is going on?
Is there anything going wrong?

Definitions of words and/or   or   When and where
cross references from my verse   did this happen?

Rewrite the verse in your own words   or   Why is this chapter in the Bible?
or personalize it.   Why did these events happen?
                                                        Why did the people act this way?

Does this verse reveal anything about God/Jesus/Holy Spirit?
Are there examples to follow or avoid? What does this chapter have to teach me?

How can I apply insights from this verse today? This week?

Notes, quotes, doodles, checklists, prayers, etc.

Deuteronomy 21

Date:

Summarize the main idea(s) in this chapter:

Verse(s) that stood out   or   Who is in this chapter?
What do they say? What do they do?

Why did I pick this verse?   or   What is going on?
Is there anything going wrong?

Definitions of words and/or   or   When and where
cross references from my verse   did this happen?

Rewrite the verse in your own words or personalize it.

or

Why is this chapter in the Bible?
Why did these events happen?
Why did the people act this way?

Does this verse reveal anything about God/Jesus/Holy Spirit?
Are there examples to follow or avoid? What does this chapter have to teach me?

How can I apply insights from this verse today? This week?

Notes, quotes, doodles, checklists, prayers, etc.

#Iwillmeditate

Deuteronomy 22

Date:

Summarize the main idea(s) in this chapter:

Verse(s) that stood out   or   Who is in this chapter?
What do they say? What do they do?

Why did I pick this verse?   or   What is going on?
Is there anything going wrong?

Definitions of words and/or   or   When and where
cross references from my verse   did this happen?

Rewrite the verse in your own words   or   Why is this chapter in the Bible?
or personalize it.   Why did these events happen?
                                                                                      Why did the people act this way?

Does this verse reveal anything about God/Jesus/Holy Spirit?
Are there examples to follow or avoid? What does this chapter have to teach me?

How can I apply insights from this verse today? This week?

Notes, quotes, doodles, checklists, prayers, etc.

#Iwillmeditate

Deuteronomy 23-24

Date:

Summarize the main idea(s) in this chapter:

Verse(s) that stood out   or   Who is in this chapter?
What do they say? What do they do?

Why did I pick this verse?   or   What is going on?
Is there anything going wrong?

Definitions of words and/or   or   When and where
cross references from my verse   did this happen?

Rewrite the verse in your own words or personalize it.

or

Why is this chapter in the Bible?
Why did these events happen?
Why did the people act this way?

Does this verse reveal anything about God/Jesus/Holy Spirit?
Are there examples to follow or avoid? What does this chapter have to teach me?

How can I apply insights from this verse today? This week?

Notes, quotes, doodles, checklists, prayers, etc.

#Iwillmeditate

Deuteronomy 25-26

Date:

Summarize the main idea(s) in this chapter:

Verse(s) that stood out   or   Who is in this chapter?
What do they say? What do they do?

Why did I pick this verse?   or   What is going on?
Is there anything going wrong?

Definitions of words and/or   or   When and where
cross references from my verse   did this happen?

Rewrite the verse in your own words   or   Why is this chapter in the Bible?
or personalize it.   Why did these events happen?
                                              Why did the people act this way?

Does this verse reveal anything about God/Jesus/Holy Spirit?
Are there examples to follow or avoid? What does this chapter have to teach me?

How can I apply insights from this verse today? This week?

Notes, quotes, doodles, checklists, prayers, etc.

#Iwillmeditate

Review and reflect #40

Date:

Review each of the last six days work. Write or list the main takeaway you got from each chapter. (Look closely at the sections "What does this reveal about God?" and "How can I apply this?")

Are there any themes showing up in this week's work?

Are there any areas God is wanting to grow my faith or trust?
Are there any insights from this week's work on how to do this?

Are there any sins God is spotlighting in my life?
Are there any insights from this week's work on how to kill these sins?

Re-read one or two of the most impactful verses from this week and turn them into a prayer. (There is room on the next pages to write it down if you want.)

How can I thank or praise God as a result of what I've learned this week?

How can I apply what I've learned this week to my life today and next week?

Where do I need His strength for today? Tomorrow? Next week?

Is there a verse from this week that I should commit to memory? Write it on the next page or on a 3x5 card to take with you to memorize.

Are there any sins I need to confess to God in prayer?

Is there anyone I need to forgive? Is there anyone I need to ask forgiveness of?

Are there any seeds of bitterness starting to take root in my heart?

Are there any fears or worries I need to lay at His feet?

#Iwillmeditate

notes, verses to memorize

prayers, doodles, etc

Deuteronomy 27

Date:

Summarize the main idea(s) in this chapter:

Verse(s) that stood out   or   Who is in this chapter?
                                         What do they say? What do they do?

Why did I pick this verse?   or   What is going on?
                                         Is there anything going wrong?

Definitions of words and/or   or   When and where
cross references from my verse   did this happen?

Rewrite the verse in your own words   or   Why is this chapter in the Bible?
or personalize it.   Why did these events happen?
                                                                  Why did the people act this way?

Does this verse reveal anything about God/Jesus/Holy Spirit?
Are there examples to follow or avoid? What does this chapter have to teach me?

How can I apply insights from this verse today? This week?

Notes, quotes, doodles, checklists, prayers, etc.

#Iwillmeditate

Deuteronomy 28

Date:

Summarize the main idea(s) in this chapter:

Verse(s) that stood out   or   Who is in this chapter?
What do they say? What do they do?

Why did I pick this verse?   or   What is going on?
Is there anything going wrong?

Definitions of words and/or   or   When and where
cross references from my verse   did this happen?

Rewrite the verse in your own words
or personalize it.

or

Why is this chapter in the Bible?
Why did these events happen?
Why did the people act this way?

Does this verse reveal anything about God/Jesus/Holy Spirit?
Are there examples to follow or avoid? What does this chapter have to teach me?

How can I apply insights from this verse today? This week?

Notes, quotes, doodles, checklists, prayers, etc.

#Iwillmeditate

Deuteronomy 29

Date:

Summarize the main idea(s) in this chapter:

Verse(s) that stood out   or   **Who is in this chapter? What do they say? What do they do?**

Why did I pick this verse?   or   **What is going on? Is there anything going wrong?**

Definitions of words and/or cross references from my verse   or   **When and where did this happen?**

Rewrite the verse in your own words
or personalize it.

or

Why is this chapter in the Bible?
Why did these events happen?
Why did the people act this way?

Does this verse reveal anything about God/Jesus/Holy Spirit?
Are there examples to follow or avoid? What does this chapter have to teach me?

How can I apply insights from this verse today? This week?

Notes, quotes, doodles, checklists, prayers, etc.

#Iwillmeditate

Deuteronomy 30

Date:

Summarize the main idea(s) in this chapter:

Verse(s) that stood out   or   Who is in this chapter?
                                              What do they say? What do they do?

Why did I pick this verse?   or   What is going on?
                                              Is there anything going wrong?

Definitions of words and/or   or   When and where
cross references from my verse   did this happen?

Rewrite the verse in your own words   or   Why is this chapter in the Bible?
or personalize it.   Why did these events happen?
                                            Why did the people act this way?

Does this verse reveal anything about God/Jesus/Holy Spirit?
Are there examples to follow or avoid? What does this chapter have to teach me?

How can I apply insights from this verse today? This week?

Notes, quotes, doodles, checklists, prayers, etc.

#Iwillmeditate

Deuteronomy 31

Date:

Summarize the main idea(s) in this chapter:

Verse(s) that stood out   or   Who is in this chapter?
What do they say? What do they do?

Why did I pick this verse?   or   What is going on?
Is there anything going wrong?

Definitions of words and/or   or   When and where
cross references from my verse   did this happen?

Rewrite the verse in your own words or personalize it.

or

Why is this chapter in the Bible?
Why did these events happen?
Why did the people act this way?

Does this verse reveal anything about God/Jesus/Holy Spirit?
Are there examples to follow or avoid? What does this chapter have to teach me?

How can I apply insights from this verse today? This week?

Notes, quotes, doodles, checklists, prayers, etc.

#Iwillmeditate

Deuteronomy 32

Date:

Summarize the main idea(s) in this chapter:

Verse(s) that stood out   or   Who is in this chapter?
What do they say? What do they do?

Why did I pick this verse?   or   What is going on?
Is there anything going wrong?

Definitions of words and/or   or   When and where
cross references from my verse   did this happen?

Rewrite the verse in your own words   or   Why is this chapter in the Bible?
or personalize it.   Why did these events happen?
                                                   Why did the people act this way?

Does this verse reveal anything about God/Jesus/Holy Spirit?
Are there examples to follow or avoid? What does this chapter have to teach me?

How can I apply insights from this verse today? This week?

Notes, quotes, doodles, checklists, prayers, etc.

Deuteronomy 33-34

Date:

Summarize the main idea(s) in this chapter:

Verse(s) that stood out   or   Who is in this chapter?
What do they say? What do they do?

Why did I pick this verse?   or   What is going on?
Is there anything going wrong?

Definitions of words and/or   or   When and where
cross references from my verse   did this happen?

Rewrite the verse in your own words or personalize it.

or

Why is this chapter in the Bible?
Why did these events happen?
Why did the people act this way?

Does this verse reveal anything about God/Jesus/Holy Spirit?
Are there examples to follow or avoid? What does this chapter have to teach me?

How can I apply insights from this verse today? This week?

Notes, quotes, doodles, checklists, prayers, etc.

#Iwillmeditate

Review and reflect #41

Date:

Review each of the last six days work. Write or list the main takeaway you got from each chapter. (Look closely at the sections "What does this reveal about God?" and "How can I apply this?")

Are there any themes showing up in this week's work?

Are there any areas God is wanting to grow my faith or trust?
Are there any insights from this week's work on how to do this?

Are there any sins God is spotlighting in my life?
Are there any insights from this week's work on how to kill these sins?

Re-read one or two of the most impactful verses from this week and turn them into a prayer. (There is room on the next pages to write it down if you want.)

How can I thank or praise God as a result of what I've learned this week?

How can I apply what I've learned this week to my life today and next week?

Where do I need His strength for today? Tomorrow? Next week?

Is there a verse from this week that I should commit to memory? Write it on the next page or on a 3x5 card to take with you to memorize.

Are there any sins I need to confess to God in prayer?

Is there anyone I need to forgive? Is there anyone I need to ask forgiveness of?

Are there any seeds of bitterness starting to take root in my heart?

Are there any fears or worries I need to lay at His feet?

Congratulations!

You did it! Great job on finishing. Look for Volume Four on Amazon to continue your journey through the Bible!

Also be sure to check out the Journal and Doodle Bible studies on Amazon and on my website www.StoneSoupforFive.com. These inductive Bible studies work through a book of the Bible and have questions to help you meditate, questions to answer, doodles, and much more.

Bible Studies

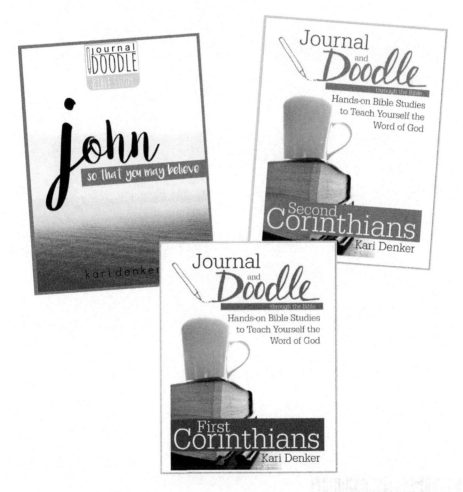

www.StoneSoupforFive.com

Made in the USA
Columbia, SC
22 June 2018